PRAYER FOR THE BULLY VICTIMS & FOR THE BULLY TOO

GRACE DOLA BALOGUN

Grace Religious Books Publishing & Distributors, Inc.
New York

Prayer For The Bully Victims And The Bully Too
By Grace Dola Balogun
Copyright © 2012 Grace Dola Balogun

Grace Religious Books Publishing & Distributors, Inc. New York. books may be ordered through booksellers or by contacting the publisher:

Grace Religious Books Publishing & Distributors, Inc.
New York
213 Bennett Avenue
New York, NY 10040

Contact Author at:
www.Gracereligiousbookspublishers.com
1-646-559-2533

All rights reserved. No part of this book may be used or reproduced by any means, graphic, electronic, or mechanical, including photocopying, recording, taping or by any information storage retrieval system without the written permission of the publisher except in the case of brief quotations embodied in critical articles and reviews.

Because of the dynamic nature of the Internet, any web addresses or links contained in this book may have changed since publication and may no longer be valid. The views expressed in this work are solely those of the author and do not necessarily reflect the views of the publisher, and the publisher hereby disclaims any responsibility for them.

The author of this book does not dispense medical advice or prescribe the use of any technique as for treatment for physical, emotional, or medical problems without the advice of a physician, either directly or indirectly. The intent of the author is only to offer information of a general nature to help you in your quest for emotional and spiritual well-being. In the event you use any of the information in this book for yourself, which is your constitutional right, the author and the publisher assume no responsibility for your actions.

Soft Cover: ISBN# 978-1-939415-11-0
Hard Cover: ISBN# 978-1-939415-12-7

Library of Congress Control Number: 2012923227

Editing and Interior Design by CBM Christian Book Marketing www.christian-book-marketing.com
Cover Design by Lisa Hainline

Printed in the United States of America
Grace Religious Books Publishing & Distributors, Inc.
New York

"A wise son brings joy to his father, but a foolish son grief to his mother. He who gathers crops in summer is a wise son, but he who sleeps during harvest is a disgraceful son. Blessings crown the head of the righteous, but violence overwhelms the mount of the wicked. The mouth of the righteous is a fountain of life, but violence overwhelms the mouth of the wicked" (Proverbs 10:1, 5-6, 11).

CONTENTS

Dedication 9
Preface 13

CHAPTER I 15
Prayer for Children Who Are Emotionally Challenged

CHAPTER II 45
Two Real Life Examples & Prayer

CHAPTER III 53
Parents' Important Duties

CHAPTER IV 65
Parents' Obligations

CHAPTER V 77
Parent's And Children's Prayers

CHAPTER VI 87
Prayer for Those Who Are Bullies

CHAPTER VII 97
August–September Review And Observation

SUMMARY 101

BIBLICAL INDEX 113

BIBLIOGRAPHY 114

ABOUT THE AUTHOR 125

DEDICATION

I dedicate this book to our God, the Father Almighty, who spoke Jesus Christ, His begotten Son into being as God's Word and Wisdom incarnate. Christ, who reflects the attributes of God the Father, just as our words and thoughts come from us and cannot be separated from us, in the same way Jesus Christ cannot be separated from the Father. Christ as the Word of God, the Speech of God, Christ is the living Word of God who lives forevermore. Christ is the wisdom of God and the power of God.

This book is written and dedicated to parents that need the knowledge that will help them to protect, correct and help their kids that are bullying other kids. This knowledge will also give the bully victims peace to study in school, the library and the freedom of mind to do his or school

homework in a positive, productive manner.

"At that time the disciples came to Jesus and asked, who is the greatest in the kingdom of heaven? He called a little child and had him stand among them. And he said: I tell you the truth, unless change and become like little children, you will never enter the kingdom of heaven. Therefore, whoever humbles himself like these children is the greatest in the kingdom of heaven. And whoever welcomes a little child like this in my name welcomes me. But if anyone causes one of these little ones who believe in me to sin, it would be better for him to have a large millstone hung around his neck and to be drowned in the depths of the seas" (Matthew 18:1-6).

I also dedicate this book to teachers, school guidance counselors and to all those who will read it. May you seek God's wisdom, acquire abundant grace, knowledge and understanding. In Christ is the righteousness of God, which is revealed from faith to faith. Believers will live in peace by faith to the point that they will give their lives to the One and only, the Word of God and God.

This book is to all the parents on Earth that see the destruction the behavior of bullying does and to those that seek after solutions for the bully kids. May peace be found for victims of the bully. May one day those that have once been a bully, come to the knowledge and understanding of the love of God in their own lives.

PREFACE

"You have heard that it was said, 'Love your neighbor and hate your enemy.' But I tell you: Love your enemies and pray for those who persecute you, that you may be sons of your Father in heaven. He causes his sun to rise on the evil and the good, and sends rain on the righteous and unrighteous. If you love those who love you, what reward will you get? Are not even the tax collectors doing that? And if you greet only your brothers, what are you doing more than others? Do not even pagans do that? Be perfect, therefore, as your heavenly Father is perfect" (Matthew 5:43-48). When someone does wrong things to us, we are not to react in a spirit of hatred, but in a way that shows that we have values that are centered in Christ and His Kingdom.

Our actions toward those who are unkind to us, such as the bully kids intentionally looking for some good kids to beat up in schools or in the neighborhood, should be

such that it might lead them to accept Christ as their Savior. Jesus Christ shows us this example when He was on the Cross. He prayed for His persecutors; Then there was Stephen who was one of the first converted Christians, when he was martyred who put Jesus' command into practice. He prayed for those who were stoning him before he died.

CHAPTER I

PRAYER FOR CHILDREN

WHO ARE EMOTIONALLY CHALLENGED

A bully is defined by different types of behavior and through various kinds of bullying others. This behavioral pattern explains the reason why some kids become bullies. We have to know that most bully kids are in a great deal of psychological, emotional rejection and loneliness that may be produced by experiencing absentee fathers or mothers. All these situations give them pain and unhappiness, as well as a reason to control their behavior in a way to make them feel powerful or worthwhile. This manipulation gives them the

confidence and motivation to continue to bully other kids. These bully kids needs prayer and reflection that will help them with their behavior. Lord we ask in your mercy to prepare the hearts, and teach us to react to the bully in a peaceful way and follow with actions, along with the right words that will lead them to You. Change them from a bully to good kids in the name of God the Father, God the Son and God the Holy Spirit, I pray, amen. Let the Bully kids know that whatever they are doing to the kids in school, they are doing it to you, our Lord and Savior Jesus Christ. In Your matchless Holy Name, amen.

Lord God Almighty, the maker of Heaven and Earth, the Sustainer, the Healer of all diseases that has plagued humanity since the beginning of the world, I hereby bring all the children of the Earth before you. I ask in Your mercy for Your healing power, stretch Your Holy hands and touch all the children in the world that are going through emotional distress. Touch their brain, their heart and restore them to the very way you created them. Wash and cleanse and purify their blood and the water in their body. Let your blood flow through their blood to purify and wash away all the emotional viruses that are causing emotional diseases in their veins and nerves. In Jesus Christ's Holy Name, I pray. Amen.

"Listen, my son, to your father's instruction and do not forsake your mother's teaching. They will be a garland to grace your head and a chain to adorn your neck" (Proverbs 1:8-9).

I pray that whatever is causing them to be troubled in their mind, Christ Jesus our Lord and Savior, You see everything; You know everything; You know the numbers of the hair on their heads. Lift all the children who are emotionally disturbed, challenged and troubled, fill them with your Holy Spirit. Bless them with a new life in Thee, a new life that will be full of the Spirit of Christ, that will produce a holy and righteous life from this Earth to Heaven. In your great and mighty Holy Name, a name above all names, I pray. Amen.

God, our Father in Heaven, full of loving- kindness and forgiveness, You are a compassionate and gracious loving God. I pray that you give all the parents in the world a sound foundation that will help parents to control the inner anger of their children that are going through anger, with feelings of wrath towards their parents, towards their siblings and towards their classmates in school. Children going through much anger these days, always think that nobody loves them. And that nobody gives them love; therefore, they have no love to give to anyone around them. They are full of hatred and jealousy towards their schoolmates in class and outside the class. They think nothing and know nothing other than how to fight and kill their friends, or their parents. Some of these children live a life of drug abuse, to include other substances that they can lay their hands on, which they feel they can derive happiness from. Lord Jesus Christ take away this type of lifestyle of drugs, bullying, hatred and anger from those children that are going through anger problems my Lord. In Your powerful, Holy Name, I pray. Amen.

Lord Jesus Christ, when you ascended to Heaven, you said all power has been given to You in Heaven and in this Earth. You have overcome the power of darkness, the power of evil, the power of violence, the power of hatred because all power belongs to You. We pray for divine deliverance from the bully children; take away the spirit of anger that is troubling them, ruling their life, driving them to hate their classmates, their parents and their siblings, and all other people around them. Take away the spirit of anger. Replace it with the spirit of love, of gentleness, of mercy, and with the spirit of joy. With your Great, Holy Name, we offer this prayer. Amen.

Lord Jesus Christ deliver bully kids with Your mighty power from Heaven. Make them a new creature. Bless them with a new spirit, a new name and a new heart. Let them live peaceful lives all the days of their life. Lord Jesus Christ deliver the bully kids from the evil spirit that is making them to think evil and do evil things to people around them where they plan evil and start fights with their classmates after school. I pray for the healing power of the anointing on all the bully kids around the world wherever they may be; fill them up with the spirit of loving-kindness, the spirit of joy and peace in the Holy Spirit. In Jesus Christ's, Holy Name, a name above all names. Amen.

Lord God Almighty Father, Son and Holy Spirit, the Holy Trinity that is forever one God, help us to teach every parent to learn and know how to talk to their children right from day one when they were born into this world. Let the parent teach their children how to love everyone around them right from birth and not wait until they are a teenager. Let Your will be automatically done in the life of all the bully kids and let your purpose be achieved in their life; turn them from evil to good, from hatred to love, from wickedness to love, from violence to peace, from unhappiness to a life of happiness and joy. Let the children be able to love their entire classmates the way they are without discrimination, or prejudice. Amen.

Lord Jesus Christ, lover of the little children, during your earthly ministry you held the little children in your arms and prayed for them and said let the little children come unto me; there is the Kingdom of Heaven. This means that everyone has to behave like a little innocent child that is clean and white as snow with no evil deeds in order to go to Heaven when they leave this Earth. If the children experience happiness from their home, teachers and friends will notice the reflection in their character. Children will reflect this happiness everywhere they go. Whether they are in school, or in their neighborhood, or doing something else, like sports, this will reflect in their behavior. I pray that parents pay more attention to their children, have more time to spend with them at home, or take them out for lunch and let them know that they love them. In the name of the Incarnate Word of God who became flesh and dwelt among us, I pray, amen.

"My son, if you accept my words and store up my commands within you, turning your ear to wisdom and applying your heart to understanding, and if you call out for insight and cry aloud for understanding, and if you look for it as for silver and search for it as for hidden treasure then you will understand the fear of the Lord" (Proverbs 2:1-5).

All children need love and want to be loved by their parents and others around them. I pray that the Board of Education will continue to research on how to be more concerned and seek help for the bully kids in each school. I pray that more counseling and therapy be available so that children can open up and let the psychologist observe and find out what is troubling the child. Sometimes these issues stem from the parents and often children are experiencing a divorce of their parents. This can cause much depression because they love both their parents and they do not want them to break up. The children suffer when their parents divorce, which is really painful to the children. If any kids joke with them, it is normal to interpret the criticism in the wrong way and this criticism might lead to a fight. Lord

Jesus Christ, I pray for the bully kids whose parents are going through divorce, a divorce in which might be alternatively the cause of the hatred and anger in their life. In Jesus Christ's Holy Name, I pray amen.

Lord Jesus Christ cast away the bitterness of the heart, mind, soul and spirit. Restore to the bully kids an inner most being with peace, love and the peace of God that surpasses all understanding to rule in all the areas of their lives. I pray Lord Jesus Christ that you turn their bitterness of heart to the heart of love and open their hearts to the good things of this world. Let them think good thoughts and feel good about themselves and others. Help them to love their classmates; cast away the Spirit of Bitterness and Jealousy from them; replace it with the Spirit of Love. Let them be able to plan good things for their lives; and teach them to be for their classmates, instead of against them, planning fighting and all other evil thinking against others. In Jesus Christ's Holy Name, I pray, amen.

Lord God Almighty, Father of mercies, wash the heart and mind of the bully kids; clean them from any evil or violent thinking. Bless them with your peace that surpasses all understanding. Touch the heart, mind and soul of their parents to give them love, show them love and to stop saying demeaning words such as, "You will never be nothing; you are dumb; other kids are better than you, etc..." All these negative words create a great impact and make children very angry. Even if even if they don't show any reaction to it, they still keep it inside them. When they go to school they will take it out on the other kids that look at them. In an instant these kids will immediately think that the other kids see what their parent say to them and see what is in them. Therefore, they are ready to take their anger out towards their parents on their innocent classmates. "Charity begins at home. . ." the Bible says; good behavior and good character begin at home. Nothing just happened; there is always a cause and effect. If the tree is good the fruit will be good. "A good tree bears good fruit" (Matthew 7:18). Lord Jesus Christ, help to us to teach the parents, the young parents and grandparents, how to use loving language to talk to their kids and their grandkids.

In the same way, adults can bring what they were going through at work home, affecting the spouse and children. Alternatively, adults can also bring to the workplace anger, and they will be angry with everybody in their office for practically no reason. In this same way, children brought whatever they were going through at home to school to everywhere they go because what is going on inside them is controlling the outside character. Bless the bully kids with your love Lord, so that they can be able to take whatever they are going through in their life with joy without violence. In Jesus Christ's Holy Name, amen.

"My son, do not forget my teaching, but keep my commands in your heart, for they will prolong your life many years and bring you prosperity, let love and faithfulness never leaves you; bind them around your neck, write them on the tablet of your heart. Then you will win favor and a good name in the sight of God and man" (Proverbs 3:1-4).

Trusting in the Lord with all our heart is the opposite of doubting God and His Word. Such trust is fundamental to our relationship with God and is based on the premise that He is trustworthy. As God's people, we can be assured that our heavenly Father loves us and will faithfully care for the problems of the bully kids in the lives of our kids. Our heavenly Father will guide us rightly; He will give us grace and keep His promises, especially in the life of the bully kids and the bully victims. All the kids that are going through difficult times in their lives with bully kids must commit their way to the Lord and trust Him that He will work on their behalf to turn the bully around to be a good kid. We must trust Him to do this for the parent, the classmates, neighbors and the community and for the

nation.

Lord Jesus Christ, lover of the little children, some parents know quite well that their children need medical checkups, or medical help, but they never have the time or money to take their children in for a medical checkup. I have worked with children and families for many years. In the past I have observed a child with erratic behavior. I have asked the parent when was the last medical checkup for this child. Some parents have answered, "Sometime ago, maybe three years ago; the child is not sick; why I should have to take my child to see the doctor and wait for hours in the hospital?" In a case like that, I have mandated the said parent to take the child to the doctor immediately and present the medical report in my office within twenty-four hours. Those reports always come back that the said child needs counseling and therapy, has behavioral problems, emotional challenges, rotting teeth and other multiple medical needs. Lord, help parents to be able to meet all their children's medical needs. In Your Holy Name, I pray. Amen.

Our heavenly Father, Father of all mercies, Sustainer of all things, be the Great Physician for the children and the kids that are in need of medical help. I bring all these children that have medical lack and neglect in their lives unto You. You alone are the architect and protector. You care for the little children, and You are the Comforter, the Counselor, the Everlasting Father and the Prince of Peace. Continuously pour out Your loving-kindness into the lives of the bully kids that have all these medical problems, especially children with emotional problems and mental health challenges, to include kids and all other medical problems mentioned that their parent's fail to care for or unintentionally neglect them, thinking that the problem will disappear or just go away. Lord, let them be able to listen to the crying of their children for help. In Jesus Christ's matchless Holy Name, amen.

Our heavenly Father, when we think of how much you love us and bless us every single day, it is so amazing that we cannot comprehend Your love. You reign in Heaven forever; Hallelujah and praises to Your Holy name. There are many children that are not happy and experiencing various kinds of difficulties. Some children are going through emotional problems, some children are going through loneliness because of the absent father or mother in the home. Some children are going through peer pressure in school or in their neighborhoods. Some are going through rejection from their own parents. All these things I bring before you Lord Jesus, bless the parents that have no love for their own children with more love for them. In Jesus Christ's Holy Name, amen.

Many children suffer and are singled out everywhere they are. Other children pick on them. Lord God Almighty, Your love for the children is incomprehensible. Let the parents love their children. They have never spent time with them. Some parents work around the clock and never stay home. Some children are living with the nanny or babysitter all day, or all week. Lord, let the parents recognize their children's needs and I pray you give them all that they need. A majority of children grow up in foster homes, kingship homes, or perhaps a relative's home, where there is no proper structure. Children are constantly competing and fighting each other for food, toys and clothing. Life does not come very easy for many children in today's society, which has resulted in the increase of bully kids in schools, not only in United States, but in all the schools in all the nations. Help us our Lord. In the name of the True God of Heaven and Earth, I pray, amen.

Lord Jesus Christ there is none like You on this Earth. I pray that you will teach each mother and father how to teach their children how to pray at bedtime before they go to sleep. Every night, whatever the parent's religion, they must have a book of prayer where the children read before going to sleep at night and pray for their classmates, neighbors, and everyone around them. Whereby they will pray for good behavior towards their teacher in school. They will pray to be able to listen to their teacher's teaching, instead of planning how to fight the other kids immediately after school. Lord, change the bully kid's mind from fighting to love. In Jesus Christ's Holy Name, amen.

Lord, I pray that you will lead these kids to live a life that will be fully committed to do good to others. You are a compassionate, loving, and forgiving Lord. Forgive all the bully kids for all the evil they have done to their classmates; bless them with a heart that is full of compassion toward everyone around them throughout their life. Lord Jesus Christ let Your light shine through the heart and mind of the bully kids to defuse the power of hatred, evil thinking, or planning evil. Bless them with great wisdom and understanding to live in this world with peace and love. Amen.

I pray Lord Jesus Christ that those parents that know You and that have been going through major problems in their lives, to the point of even some of them that committing suicide because they cannot take it anymore. They cannot live with the threat of their own children every day, threatening to kill them. I pray that you fill them up with your strength and power. Make them to be strong to fight the evil in the lives of their children. Let them continue to look for help for their children. Do not let them give up looking for help for their children. Make them to be ready at all times to stand alongside their children and fight

the evil that is troubling them. Let them feel and see Your compassionate presence, that You brought to their life when they pray to you O'Lord. In Jesus Christ's Holy Name, amen.

Lord Jesus Christ, You are the light, which defuses darkness and restores inner peace. Deliver the parents of the bully kids from the darkness, arrogance, ignorance, jealousy, envy and from all the evils that plague the minds and hearts of the young children in the world. Lord Jesus Christ You are the wisdom of God; and You are the power of God to those who believe in You; take care of all the anxiety and insecurity experienced by the bully kids and their parents. Let them hear and read Your Word daily. Even though they are going through pains in many areas of their lives, to include loss and multiple failures in their lives; be their hope of glory for them; enable them to see God in all the problems and circumstances they might be going through. Let them know that you are in total control and You will bring it to pass in due time. In Jesus Christ's Holy Name, amen.

God Almighty Father, Son and the Holy Spirit: You are the One and only God of possibilities; nothing is impossible for you to do on this Earth and in Heaven. You are the beginning and the end, the life, the truth, and the only way to Heaven. Let all Your creation worship You in spirit and in truth with singleness of heart. Bless them with unmerited favor, which is your grace. By grace we are saved, not through any work. It is through our faith in Jesus Christ that we became a new creature. You are a God of love who listens to the prayers and answers prayer if You know that whatever we ask in prayer is good for us and that it will bring glory to Your Holy Name. Do not let Your mercies fail on the bully kids and their parents. Your faithfulness is great. Your loving-kindness is incomparable. Your counsel and encouragement always helps us in times of problems and adversities. In Jesus Christ's Holy Name, I pray, amen.

 Bless all the bully kids with the power of Your Spirit that will enable them and help them to overcome all their troubles, problems, and all what is lacking in their lives. Let them know that You are bigger than the problems they face every day such as living with a parent that does not love them, nor care for them. Let them be able to exercise their trust in Your goodness and Your loving-kindness. Let them know Your will for their lives. Some bully kids behave badly in order to get help from their parents; some will go and sell drugs for the big-brother of their neighborhood, which makes their life more difficult and miserable because of the threat they go through with the big-brothers that are using them to sell drugs. All these parents do not know what their kids are doing. Kids do not want to constantly ask their parents for money whenever they need money for a school project. They take things into their own hands by reaching out to the neighborhood big-brothers. They go from worse to worst because they will not have time to go to school or do their school work, nor do they have any peace. Therefore, when they go to school, they want to cause trouble with other kids so that they can give them a suspension to get them out of school. When

that happens they have more time to work with the big-brother by selling drugs. Lord Jesus Christ, protect the bully kids from their big-brothers that are using them for their own gain. In Jesus Christ's Holy Name, amen.

Lord Jesus Christ, expose the big-brothers of the neighborhood that are making the bully-kids sell drugs for them. They are creating hatred and violence in their lives. They threaten the children and tell them that they are going to hurt, or kill their parents so that they can continue working for them. Lord Jesus Christ, you see everything. You know everything. Help us to expose all this evil that the bully kids are going enduring in their neighborhood that has created a huge effect on them in school, making them insecure in school, and causing them to exercise violent behavior in school towards their classmates. It also makes them not to value their own life and they sometimes commit suicide. In Jesus Christ's Holy Name, I pray, amen.

Lord God Almighty, protect the bully kids and all other kids in the neighborhood against the big-brothers that are using them in so many ways, to include all forms of sexually immoralities. Sometimes they take them to ride the train and make them walk around begging for money. One day, as I was on the train, this beautiful kid was dancing, jumping up and down and before we knew it, he knocked his chest on the train pole. He was unable to breath properly and an ambulance was called to take him to the hospital. Lord God, Almighty Father, Son and the Holy Spirit, protect the kids from the big-brother that is making them panhandle on the train and on the street of the big cities. In Jesus Christ's Holy Name, amen.

CHAPTER II

TWO REAL LIFE EXAMPLES & PRAYER

When I was working with the children, I have a client that leaves home every morning on time, although her children were not attending school as they were supposed to. The parents of these children were not aware that the children were not going to school. The man that was hired in the neighborhood to help them with their school homework before the parents' came back from work was taking them to another borough to dance and beg for money all day. The children would not come home until Twelve Midnight, and the mother asked him why. He always told the mother that he engaged her kids with extra studies. Not until the school called educational neglect on the mother and were

ready to take the mother to court, did the parents cry and ask their children why they were not going to school? They said that the big-brother told them not to tell her and that if they let their mother know where they were going, that their mother would be in trouble.

Lord Jesus Christ, I pray that you protect the children from the neighborhood men that the parents are using to help their children. It is unfortunate that even though they get paid for the service that they agreed to do, they turn the children to a life of begging, which creates a big mess. They are greedy for money and have turned the lives of children they are supposed to help into problem children. Expose all the big- brothers in the neighborhood, those who have carried out all these evil deeds against the children in the neighborhood. In the name of Your Son, Jesus Christ, amen.

Gracious, loving, Spirit of God, the Holy Spirit, Heaven Dove, arrive with your great light and comfort from above the hearts and minds of the bully kids that are going through troubles from the neighborhood big-brothers. Be Thou their Guardians, and guide them; keep them safe, let the big-brothers in the neighborhood stop making their life miserable; stay close to these children who are suffering innocently for what they do not understand. They are going to jail for somebody else for practically what they have no knowledge of. Lead them out of the hands of the wicked and selfish big-brothers. Lord I pray that You have mercy on all the school children in their neighborhood, and in school. In Jesus' Holy Name, amen.

Lord Jesus Christ, our Father in Heaven, let the people of this Earth know that there are times in some children's lives when they stray away and are lost into the world. This happens when they stray away from You. They have lost their path to reach you, or they don't know You at all. Let my prayer reach all the children in this world wherever they may be. My prayers are for the children who are lost and for those that are not able to reach out to you in their troubles and problems. These children are in need of a Savior. They need You, Jesus Christ, in their lives. They are in need of guidance; they are in need of your mercy and loving-kindness. They are in need of Your infinite love. Provide all that they need to live a peaceful life. Give them a life of joy and happiness and help them to live a meaningful life that will help others. Teach them to not hurt others around them. In Your great and Mighty Holy Name, I pray. Amen.

The psalmist says:

"Remember, O Lord, your great mercy and love, for they are from of old. Remember not the sins of my youth and my rebellious ways, according to your love remember me, for you are good, O'Lord" *(Psalm 25:6-7).*

The psalmist is saying that during the time of youth, rebellion is the way many youth choose to live their lives; such is the way that the bully kids have chosen to live their life. God understands this because of the circumstances of the environment that the children are living in, which have a great impact in their lives. Lord, help the parents of the kids that are going through a rebellious time to understand the stage of helplessness that their children are going through because of the actions of their kids. Lord Jesus, help the parents to transform all the anger, bitterness, frustration and hatred that the child might be going through into Your great good for them, so that they will see Your loving-kindness that never ceases in their lives. In Your mighty Holy Name, I pray, amen.

You are the God of comfort; comfort the parents by healing their broken hearts. Let them continue to have hope in You and to believe that You have the power to turn the bully kids around for the better. Let the bully kids see what they are doing to themselves before it is too late. When they plan to destroy another kid's life, let them come to the knowledge that they are destroying their own life. Let them think about what they are going to do before they do it because after it has been done, it will create a big problem that they cannot repair. Lord God Almighty, help the bully kids to do the right thing at all times; restore peace into their lives and let them know that you care for them. You want them to live a peaceful life. Comfort the hearts of the parents of the kids that are bullying people around. Let the bully kids know that they are bringing shame to their parents and to their own name. Help us to forgive the sin of rebellious kids our Lord. In your Mighty Holy Name, I pray. Amen.

"A wise son brings joy to his father, but a foolish son grief to his mother. Blessings crown the head of the righteous, but violence overwhelms the mouth of the wicked" *(Proverbs 10:1, 6).*

CHAPTER III

PARENT'S IMPORTANT DUTIES

I pray that parents introduce their kids to know God's ways and God's love. It is possible for the people of this Earth and believers to know something about God's most important activities, most important salvation and miracles, but to never really know God personally, intimately or understand God's ways, such as the role of testing and hardship. Waiting on the Lord, humility and brokenness are some of God's ways. Prayer and fasting, faith, wisdom, guidance and perseverance are all God's instruments that lead children to a loving environment. A life of purity with relation to spiritual authority and maturity are monumental.

The basic principles for knowing God's ways in this world are the following: We must have a sincere desire to be led into God's righteous ways and the truth of God's Word. We must be anxious and eager to put our hope in the Lord Jesus Christ all the days of our life. We must humble ourselves to submit to God, commit ourselves to godly living and the fear of the Lord. We must lead our children in any problems they are going through the light of God by seeking the heavenly Father for our children's eternal life.

We must know that the Lord is our refuge in times of trouble. Before the mountains were brought forth, or ever formed, the Earth according to His Word, God is from everlasting to everlasting and is caring, comforting, sharing His Holy words by sending messages to parents on how to care for their children. Parents must faithfully meet the needs of the their children, in that they should seek medical care and financially support the needs of their children. Parents must not have kids if they know they have no time to take good care of them.

Children are too precious to God. It would be better to stay in Heaven with Him instead of the parent that

brought them into this world and has no time to care of them. Children must not be left on the street everyday in the care of a wicked neighbor, or kept locked in the home alone to do any evil thing they can think of because there is no supervision. If the children know God at the beginning of their lives, they will be able to cope with life's problems.

Adversities such as divorce, domestic violence, rejection from friends and relatives in their lives will not necessarily result into bitter behavior from children, or change children from good behavior to bad behavior. I pray that they grow up and realize not to blame God for every bad thing that is happened in their life or in the entire world. With God, they will know that God will always lead them to the point that they will receive God's favor in their lives.

Lord Jesus Christ, shower Your loving- kindness to the bully kids and their parents with the flame of love that never ends. Surround them with your power of the indwelling of the Holy Spirit. You are the One and only. You are the God of light who has immortality in the light and no darkness can comprehend. Look down from Heaven and heal all the bully kids; perform Your miracle in their lives. Exhibit your loving-kindness in their lives and extend Your love in every detail in their lives. In the name of the ever living Lord, I pray, amen.

Lord Jesus, You are our great intercessor in Heaven. I pray for the bully kids, a prayer that can never be uttered. Drive away any evil spirit from them and let them live a normal life that you require and approve. Let them see Your great light and follow the light. Let them forever stay in the light. May Your light of great compassion and mercy encompass their lives. In Your Holy Name, I pray, amen.

Lord God Almighty, children are the greatest gift for the people on this Earth, but they don't know it. It is a joy when a child is born and looks just like the father or the mother. There is no joy that can replace that joy in the heart of the parents. If the child has any problems, it is the parents' responsibility to care for their children and make sure that their children are happy at all times, to include meeting all the needs of their kids. When a child is feeling depressed, distressed, and looks very sad, parents must make a diligent effort to see that the child opens up to them in whatever is troubling the child. Some parents, once they have a room for their children, and a television in their kid's room, they don't want to know what is going on with the children.

This has resulted in many children that have watched pornography, violent movies, and all various kinds of sexually immoralities on the television and the parent's are not aware of it. Some parents did not even know that their children were not doing their school homework until the school calls them and informs them about the child's grades. Children that are going through the problem of neglect by parents always feel helpless and frustrated.

When they go to school, they scream and yell at the teacher and their fellow students. They even may be planning how to kill everybody and kill themselves.

Lord Jesus Christ, manifest your power into the hearts, minds and souls of all the children; pour out Your love and wisdom into their lives. Bring great healing anointing to heal the pain that the child mighty be going through. Help them to become loving and wise kids, full of great knowledge and understanding that will take them from evil to good, that will help them to live holy lives and godly lives. I bring these children to the front of Your Throne and to Your Throne room, may mercy be on these children every single day, as Your mercies are new every morning. In Your matchless Holy Name, I pray. In the name of Jesus Christ, I pray, amen.

Lord Jesus Christ, You love all the children of this world; pour down Your healing to the bully kids so that can be free from anger, bitterness, hatred, jealousy and all the other things that constitute violent character. Let the fullness of Your presence be known in their life. Manifest Yourself and stay by your children; be the God of all mercies and comfort through their lives. Keep them to be aware of Your loving presence. Bless them with your healing power and comfort their parents. Amen.

O' Lord God, we call on to You to help us raise the bully kids; You are our great protector. Come quickly and help the parents to take care of the bully kids. Help them to understand that life in the way of the Lord is best; help them to bear affliction with patience and strength. Bless them Holy Father with good health, do not forsake them or leave them. Let Your full presence be known in their lives. Show them Your way; for Your way is true and bless them with the assurance of your loving-kindness and Your Kingdom. Help all the parents and teach them how to pray for their children. Make them better children for their parents. In the name of Your one and only Son, I pray. Amen.

"A good name is more desirable than great riches; to be esteemed is better than silver or gold. Rich and poor have this in common; The Lord is the Maker of them all" (Proverbs22:1-2).

Come Holy Spirit of God, the comforter and the Counselor, let your bright light shine in the hearts, minds and souls of the bully kids. Diffuse the darkness of their heart; open their eyes and kindle their faith, wash away their fears and turn them around for the better. In the name of the Almighty Father and Son and the Holy Spirit, I pray, amen.

CHAPTER IV

PARENTS OBLIGATION

The main reason that children are behaving badly today is because parents are not encouraging their kids to live a respectable life; they did not teach them to value themselves and value other classmates' values and to respect them. There is no proper communication between parents and kids. Parents do not realize that it is their sole responsibility to raise their children, in a way that they will be a good person in the community and in the nation.

Even some Christian parents go to church and leave their children at home. One of the greatest sins of God's people in the Old Testament was the failure of the father or mother to love their sons and daughters. Parents are to love

their children dearly, so much so that they are constantly teaching them the ways and the commandments of God. By actively participating in the life of their children, their hearts will be fully consecrated and the children will fully return to good behavior.

This is a clear statement and it is one of the key goals of the Gospel, which is to re-establish God's presence, awareness of Him and His Will. In order for the family to create a good relationship between the father, mother and their children, through preaching of repentance and the Lordship of Christ, the father and mother will become dedicated to their children in a character of righteousness. When parents fail to love their children, spend time with them and teach them God's words, with righteousness and holiness, parents fail to teach their children to respect self and to respect their classmates and other people. Children are not taught value of self, and to value their classmates, and other people. Children must be taught respect for what is important to their classmates, respect every one's lifestyle, and to value individuals as they are. Parents should correct with love and children should be ready to be corrected. Children need to be taught

to value every one's standard of living, race, culture and to respect others regardless of nationality.

Scripture says, "He will turn the hearts of the fathers to their children, and the hearts of the children to their fathers" (Malachi 4:6a). John the Baptist preached about this to the people in the Old Testament. There can be no blessing from God or abundant life in the Spirit, if God's people do not make family, and most importantly, authority, love and faithfulness absolute priorities in the church. The purity and righteousness of the family home must be maintained; otherwise, children will fail whenever they are outside the home, or even in the home.

The one most responsible for accomplishing this task is the father of the family. If the father is not in the home, then the mother takes full responsibility of nurturing the children. Parents must love their children by constantly praying for them in every circumstance every day. Spending time with them, pointing out the ungodly ways of the world, and diligently teaching them God's Word, righteousness and godly peaceful living. This is a parent's obligation in this world of violence. Therefore, it is the sole responsibility of parents, both the father and the

mother. They are to give their children instruction and correction that will help their children restructure their behavior anywhere they may be in their life. Parents should set examples for their children by staying away from any form of violence, wrath and anger especially domestic violence between a mother and father. If parents are living a peaceful life, it is an automatic inheritance children will follow the same step. If parents value and respect their children and other people around them, the children will do the same. If parents are caring more for their children's well-being in a godly way, children will do the same. It is therefore, the responsibility of the parents to show their children the way of salvation, to be concerned for their life and how they can be saved and be able to enter the eternal life, which God has provided for those who believe in Him. It is the responsibility of both parents to bring their children up and prepare them for lives that are pleasing to God.

Biblically and spiritually training of children by the parents is the way of God. According to the Christian who is nurturing and raising their children, the heart of the parents' must be turned to the hearts of the children in

order to bring the heart of the children to the heart of the Lord. Parents should not show favoritism between one child or another. They must encourage, as well as correct. They must discipline only when discipline is needed when the children intentionally does something wrong that can endanger their lives. This must be done in union with each parent and each parent must supply love to their children with a heart of compassion, kindness, humility, gentleness and patience.

With all this analysis, in order to help the bully kids and in order for our prayers to be answered so that good results will come from our prayers for the bully kids, we must pray for the parents, and also let the parents know that they need to do their own part.

It is the parents' responsibility to take full charge by spending more time at home with their children and also by communicating with their children, not just to put a television in their rooms, but to monitor what kind of movie or shows that they are watching. "That you may tell your children and grandchildren how I dealt harshly with the Egyptians and how I performed many signs among

them and that you may know that I am the Lord" (Exodus 10:2).

From time to time in the Old Testament when God spoke, He always wanted us to communicate with our children and grandchildren. God always showed great concern for the children in order for them to know who He is in order to be able to acknowledge what He has done for them. He wants children to come to the realization of His love for them and accept Him as their God in faith and with obedience.

God chose Abraham with one purpose, that he should teach his children to keep the way of the Lord. He also commanded the Israelites to be diligent in teaching their children the words of the Lord. And in the same way, God is teaching us today to teach our children in the right way and not to neglect them, but teach them to live peaceful lives that God commanded every people in the world to live.

God knew that if parents fail in this solemn duty, the next generation of the people in the world would turn to more and more violent lives. They will not know God and His righteous way or live godly lives. Wickedness and

hatred will continue to rise more and more. Bully kids will continue to increase until none will want to go to school. Schools will be filled with more security devices up to the point that school children will not have freedom to study peacefully in school. "Children, obey your parents in the Lord, for this is right. Honor your father and mother which is the first commandment with a promise – that it may go well with you and you may enjoy long life on the earth" (Ephesians 6:1-3). Some Christian children remain under the parental guidance and control until they become part of another family unit, which means until they are married, or become adults.

When they are children, they must be taught to follow rules and regulations with a set pattern where they obey the rules and honor and value their parents by being obedient. They are brought up in the training and instruction of the Lord. This should be apply to all the children growing up in a household, to obey their parents' instructions so that they can behave well in schools and everywhere they may be. Whether their parents are there or the parents are not in that place at that particular time,

they must remember their parents' instructions and behave very well to others around them.

There are many times that the love of some parents can be very cold, as cold as ice cubes and bitter gall towards their children. They don't have time and money to spend on their children's needs. Parents are struggling with their own earthly problems and without the faith and the love of God, parents can become frozen and cease to show love for their children. This attitude can easily cause their children to therefore bully other kids at school, or in the neighborhood. I am confident that the way some parents can sustain their love for their kids and others, will be to keep his or her faith alive with prayer.

The Book of Proverbs is very helpful to parents, it says: *"Listen, my sons, to a father's instruction pay attention and gain understanding. I give you sound learning, so do not forsake my teaching when I was a boy in my father's house still tender, and an only child of my mother, he taught me and said, lay hold of my words with all your heart; keep my commands and you will live. Get wisdom, get understanding; do not forget my words or swerve*

from them. Do not forsake wisdom, and she will protect you. Love her, and she will watch over you. Wisdom is supreme, therefore get wisdom. Though it cost all you have, get understanding" (Proverbs 4:1-7).

King Solomon, the author of the Book of Proverbs, had learned about God's ways from his father and was now passing instructions on to his sons. God wants true godliness and commitment to His ways to be learned primarily through the teaching of parents and the example provided in the home.

The wisdom of God is very essential to live a meaningful and godly life. Therefore, parents must seek it above all things for their children. However, to attain such wisdom is not easy, for it is given only to those who diligently pay the price for it. Wisdom comes in two ways: (1) Through God's instruction; through the revelatory instruction a person may experience knowledge of God that makes possible spiritual transformation and God's kind of wisdom. The fear of the Lord that motivates us to turn away from evil is the beginning of true wisdom. (2)

Spiritual diligence: Wisdom is for the person who sees its value and therefore diligently seeks wisdom. The wise person learns from instruction and from God's discipline; accepts God's commands, listens to the godly counsel of parents and others. This person with wisdom also treasures wisdom as more valuable than silver, gold or precious jewels.

Christ is the supreme manifestation of the wisdom of God, thus, the Old Testament exhortation is equivalent to a call to commit our lives to Jesus Christ. We must turn from sin and self to Him, sacrificing all that is necessary in order to follow Him as His disciples. Wisdom brings life and is life. To live as God has designed brings a good and joyful life, normally a longer physical life, to include a moral and spiritual life with the hope of life after death.

CHAPTER V

PARENTS AND CHILDREN'S PRAYER

P arents and children prayer: Jesus Christ our Lord and Savior, I give you thanks that I awake this morning and see your great light shining above. You are the only one that kept me safe through the night when I was asleep. To You only I lifted my hands and direct my prayer to this morning. Keep the bully kids away from me, keep me from sin, and let the bully kids in my class that is planning to beat me after school, turn him to love me and to plan good things for me and turn him to be my best friend. Keep me safe and protect me from the violence of the bully kids, and protect other kids in my school as well who does not have peace from the bully

kids. In the name of the Incarnate Word of God who became flesh, I pray, amen.

Parents must teach and engage their kids in prayer. Victims must pray for the bully themselves. Parents must teach their kids to be happy with how God created them and lift them up to let them learn to value themselves in the neighborhood, in the community, in school, in the sports arena and anywhere they are. Let the parents teach their kids the love of God, and to understand that God loves them unconditionally. He surrounds them with His angels at all times and the Spirit of Jesus Christ dwells in them. We pray that parents lead the kids to the way of salvation; whereby, they will be able to pray for the bully kids who bully them. Innocent kids need to approach the Throne of Grace and ask for great wisdom, knowledge and understanding. Children who are under the threat of bully kids should ask for God's protection from bully kids. I pray that the spirit of the power of God will fill them and wash away fears, anger and timidity from them. May the spirit of love help them to overcome the threat and the violence of the bullies in their lives. Parents must pray together with their kids so that they can overcome the

problems together and pray that the school authorities will take the threat of the bullies seriously every time the victim reports the bully kid's threats. The school authority must do all what is necessary to protect the victim from the bully kids.

We pray that the Spirit of God takes over and solves the problems in a miraculous way. We pray that both the bully and the victim get the help they need. Parents and innocent kids must pray for the salvation of the bully kids, so that they will be touched and anointed by the Spirit of the Most High God. In the name of Jesus Christ, I pray, amen.

Look upon my child's weakness O Lord, gracious Father, lay Your hands on him and make him a strong person that is full of wisdom and understanding. Make him what You want him to be for Your glory. Supply all his needs, physically and spiritually, day and night; supply the desire and ability to be able to go to school without any problems from the bully kids. Make every moment a precious time in his life. Help him in all the areas of his life; anoint him with the spirit of anointing so that he can be able to stay away from the bully kids and keep bully kids away from him. In Your glorious Holy Name, I pray, amen.

The Bible says:

"Sons are a heritage from the lord, children a reward from him. Like arrows in the hands of a warrior are sons born in one's youth. Blessed is the man whose quiver is full of them. The will not be put to shame when they contend with their enemies in the gate" (Psalm 127:3-5).

In the Old Testament, a large family was considered a blessing, while not having children was considered a curse. Under the New Covenant, the presence of many children is not necessarily evidence of divine favor, nor is their absence to be viewed as a curse. A large family may be a misfortune if the children are not properly cared for and brought to salvation in Christ. Having children can be a blessing if one dedicates his or her life and time to the Lord's service. Children must be viewed as a gifts of God requiring wise and faithful stewardship. Only as the Lord's ways and commands are accepted, taught and followed by parents, the children will experience God's full blessing.

Do not let us forget that sons and daughters are a heritage from your Lord Jesus; they are the fruit of the womb, a great reward for you. They are just like arrows in the hand of a warrior that born in one's youth. Blessed is the man who fills his house with them. Lord Jesus, with this revelation in our mind, bless us with more and more children from You. In Your matchless Holy Name, amen.

I call upon Thee Lord, for You will hear me and answer my prayers. Show Your marvelous loving-kindness, O'Lord. You are One that saves our children by Your right hand. I ask that You save those who put their trust in You from all those bully kids that rise up against them. Keep those innocent kids safe today and forever as the apple of Your eye. Hide their face and all their being from bully kids that are planning to fight with them after school. Hide them under the shadow of Your wings, protect them, guide, and keep them safe. Hear our prayer Lord; let Your great glory shine upon them so that they will not be able to come near them. I pray this in the precious Name of Jesus Christ. Amen.

Lord God Almighty, You are the same from everlasting to everlasting, our Father in Heaven, the Father of all mercies, and the Sustainer of all things. You care for Your children even before you put them in their mother's womb. Stretch Your holy hands and surround Your children from all the bully kids that are terrorizing other kids around in the schoolyard and planning to fight against some others. You surrounded the people of Israel in the wilderness. Our schools are now like a wilderness because of the threat of the bully kids. Be our guardian from the school bullies. Control the bully so that they don't follow up after school. Most importantly, send help to the bully kids in many ways that will stop them from bullying to being loving kids. In Jesus Christ's name, I pray. Amen.

CHAPTER VI

PRAYER FOR THOSE WHO ARE BULLIES

I call upon Thee Lord, for You will hear me my Lord, and my prayers. Show Your marvelous loving-kindness; O'Lord, You that save Your children by Your right hand, save those who put their trust in You; save me from all these bully kids that rise up against me. Keep me today and forever as the apple of Your eye. Hide my face and all of me from bully kids that are planning to fight with me after school. Hide me under the shadow of Your wings, protect me, guide me and keep me safe. Make Your great glory to shine upon me so that they will not be able to come near me. I pray in the precious, Holy Name of Jesus. Amen.

You are the same from everlasting to everlasting, our Father in Heaven, Who is the Father of all mercies and Sustainer of all things. You care for Your children even before you put them in their mother's womb. Stretch Your Holy hands and surround Your child from all the bully kids that are running around the schoolyard to fight some other students. Surround them with pillar of fire, just as You surrounded the people of Israel in the wilderness. You are my Deliverer, O' Lord; deliver me from bully kids. In the name of God the Father, God the Son and God the Holy Spirit, I pray, amen.

Our schools are now like the wilderness because of the threat of the bully kids. Be my guardian from the school bully; control the bully so that they don't follow me after school. Most importantly, I ask that You send help to the bully kids in so many ways that they will stop from bullying others and learn to love kids instead. In Jesus Christ's Holy Name, I pray, amen.

"Do not envy wicked men, do not desire their company; for their hearts plot violence, and their lips talk about making trouble. By wisdom a house is built, and through understanding it is established; through knowledge its rooms are filled with rare and beautiful treasures" (Proverbs 24:1-4).

Our heavenly Father, in your great mercy and infinite love, call all the bully kids unto You. Bless them with your unfailing love that will change them from bully kids to gentle kids. This will change them from haters of good kids, to lovers of good kids. Show them Your love so that they can love other kids through the love You pour upon them. In Your matchless Holy Name, I pray, amen.

Our Father in Heaven, let the bully kids think about what they are doing to themselves before they start problems by beating other kids. Let them know that they are messing up their own life. They are creating a big problem to themselves and for their parents. Let them think and know that they are messing up their career in life by allowing evil to rule their lives, instead of good. Let them know that they can easily spend the rest of their life in prison if they beat any child to death. In Jesus Christ's Holy Name, I pray. Amen.

Our Lord and Savior, I pray for the bully not only in my school, but in all the schools all over the world. Let them be still and know that there is God who looks down and sees everything they are doing to another parent's child; help them to stop their evil deeds. Help us to speak to the bully kids our Lord. In Your Holy Name, I pray. Amen.

Lord Jesus Christ our Lord and Savior, as I wake up this morning let today be a peaceful day for me and for all the other students, including the bully kids. Let their parents meet all their needs; let them be happy without thinking of fighting. Erase all the symptoms of fighting from their spirit, soul and body. Erase all forms of violent from their minds. Erase all forms of evil thinking from their blood, wash them clean from any form of evil, violence and anger from the water, bones and flesh of their body. Pray through me for the bully kids everywhere in the world. In Your great Holy Name, I pray. Amen.

Lord God Almighty, the Creator of Heaven and Earth, the sea and everything that dwells in it. I pray that You work with the bullying among the school children, and bring righteousness in all the schools and neighborhoods of all the nations where school kids are experiencing bullying of innocent kids. I pray that our Lord and Savior puts a stop to the oppression of the bully kids in all the schools. I pray that all the kids love each other and study with peace with the understanding of peace. In Your matchless Holy Name, amen.

Lord God Almighty, make the bully kids a clean vessel; let them live to be good and live a good and gentle life at home with their parents and at school with their fellow classmates. Take away all kinds of drugs from them. Take away all thoughts of fighting from them. Renew the bully kid's mind, soul and body. Continuously wash them clean from all evil every day. In Jesus Christ's Holy Name, a name above all names, I pray. Amen.

I pray for the peace of God and for good health for the bully kids. Let the parents of the bully kids seek medical help for their kids in order to know why they get angry for any little thing, why they are not happy, and why they are so bitter. They are full of bitterness towards other kids in school. Let their parents find out what they are going through and if there is a medical mental disorder, or find out if they are mentally challenged. Let parents of bully kids take time to care for their children, medically and physically to find out what is their kid's problems and give them wisdom to know how to cure it. In Jesus Christ's Holy Name. Amen.

CHAPTER VII

AUGUST - SEPTEMBER REVIEW AND OBSERVATION

From the beginning of the month of August to September when the school starts we need to pray for all the school kids because many kids are very scared to go back to school. There are some kids who find the first day of school to be like as if they are entering back into burning flame of fire because of bullying kids. While some bullying kids find the first day of school to be as if they first start their operations, and they might even be very excited about all the evil things they are going to do to innocent kids who are victims.

There is much severe bullying from these kids and for various reasons. It begins from picking on weight, or any form of disability of the victim, sometimes they might pick on the victims looks, height, nationality, culture, or either parent that is either too rich or too poor. Most of the time there are many suicide victims around the beginning of the school because it is too much to be going through the abuse every day and they might not see any changes or have any hope. I pray every day that suicides from the bullying victims are reduced to minimum or completely eradicated from schools all over the nations. We need to pray at the beginning of each new school year for all the children. I pray that the God of all, the God of all mercies and the Creator of all things, all races, cultures and nationalities keep all the children safe. You are the One and only, and the sustainer of all things. Amen.

We pray that this school year will be peaceful for those kids that are going through emotional stress and struggling as victims of bullying by bully kids. I pray for those innocent kids who are going through verbal abuse, or threats, enduring beatings, monetary bullying and for those also that are experiencing ceaselessness, or nonstop teasing. I pray for those who are going through physical abuse from bully kids. Strengthen them our Lord and Savior, make them strong so that they can learn how to ignore the bully kids this year. Teach them how to study in peace with the bully. Help us to change the bully to peaceful kids.

We also pray for the bullied kid's parents who feel that they cannot change their kids or for those parents who feel they cannot tell them to stop. Make them strong so that they can come to a realization that their kids cannot continue to live a life of violence. Let the bully kids, as well as the parents, understand that there is always consequences for good and bad behavior. Let them be able to protect their kids and talk their kids out of trouble by constantly talking to them. Let the parents of bully kids show their kids love, affection, and let them have hope that they can show the teacher that they can be good. Let the

teachers ignore the cry of the bully in the classroom, lunch room and during gym or sports practice.

SUMMARY

We have to look at the life of bully kids. A bully kid gets up to go to school in the morning, while waiting for a bus at the bus stop, the bus may not show up on time. He will turn around and take it on the other school kids waiting for bus. He will start picking on other kids at the bus stop by calling them all sorts of ugly names that he can think of. He might even get in the other kid's faces, threatening to beat him or her up.

Bullying can turn into emotional distress that can lead to emotional problems that might not be healed for the life of the victim. This abuse is an intentional violation of other kid's peace of mind. If any children around you is going through bullying at school or at the bus stop or anywhere on the way going home, or at school, there are

many ways to help him or her to cope with day to day bullying in the neighborhood or at school.

Bullying is what the parents should freely talk to their kids about and let them know that it can be ignored or cured. Bullying is an internal act of tormenting someone physically and/or verbally. The abuse may also result in psychological abuse. All these intentional acts can also result in hitting, name calling in an ugly manner, threats, mocking to extortion of bully kids often demanding money from innocent kids, or taking away the innocent kid's lunch money from them. Sometimes the bully kids will take kid's winter coats, or some valuable items from their classmates. They might even demand certain things from the innocents kid's family or ask for a treasured possession from the kids that they are bullying.

Another form of bullying is when bully kids carry some untrue stories against the innocent kids, thereby blackmailing the other classmates. This type of rumor can occur in the form of an e-mail, type written papers, text messages, instant messages, Facebook, all in order to hurt the feelings of innocent kids.

Parents must take the bullying activities seriously and go to any extent to help their kids. Bullying has serious effects on innocent victims, with painful impacts on the kids because bullying might contribute to suicide and other tragedies. Even to the point that some kids may bring guns to the school to shoot other kids.

Sometimes bullying kids are bullies for so many reasons; sometimes they pick on kids because they see that the other kids are very weak emotionally or physically. In most cases bully kids are bigger and stronger than their victims. The bully just wants to be in control of the weaker kids. Sometimes bullies torment their victims and other innocent kids because they are not happy kids.

We have to realize that most, if not ninety-five percent of our television shows promote bullying. Television shows portray angry behavior with screaming, yelling and ridicule of family members. Also domestic violence where the father and mother scream at each other is prevalent on television. Parents should always find other means that will help their children to open up about bullying to their teachers, school guidance counselors, friends or family.

If your child finally opens up about bullying, support him or her, no matter how sad you may be. Some kids feel reluctant to talk about the bully's torment in their lives because they feel it is too embarrassing and shameful. Due to this they might not want their parents to know; also, they might feel that they should be able to handle it. They always feel that if the bully kids find out they told their parents that they might increase their bullying on him or her. Some kids have the feeling that if their parents knew, they may tell them to fight back, which creates more anxiety for them.

Parents and older siblings should take it seriously if the bullying is getting worse. It is very important to inform the bullying kids' parents so that they will be able to help their own kids by finding out what is causing their kids to bully other kids. School teachers and school guidance counselors should be involved, as well as a psychologist and the school principal for the bully kids in order to find out whether the bully kids are experiencing mental problems of any form.

It would be advisable to transfer the bully kids to another school or have them be homeschooled if he or she

continues to bully the kids. Sometimes, parents might get the court involved with bully kids, whereby, if bullying kids do not stop the abuse, they might be placed in a therapeutic facility for more thorough help to ensure the safety of the child.

The main important way to help the bullying is to provide a strategy that will help the kids to cope with the bullying in school every day. This can also include clinical observations and practical applications that will help the victims restore his or her self-esteem, self-worth and integrity, so that they can regain their dignity and value of who they are in life.

Kids that were getting bullied should learn how to ignore the bullying, pay them no mind and pretend that whatever they were saying does not affect them. Reacting by crying or looking upset or sad will make the bully to continue their bad behavior against an innocent victim.

The bullying victim should behave bravely by walking smart, firmly and clearly confront the bullying to stop and act as if uninterested as to whatever the bully is saying to them. By ignoring the bullying, it will show that the kids do not care and the bullying will stop his or her

attitude and look for something else to do. Telling the teacher, principal will also help to stop bullying quickly as well. If the bully is asking you for money don't give it to him or her. Go and tell your parents, and the parent will tell the legal authority.

Parents should introduce their kids to other good kids that will change their self-worth, and perhaps this will help them to build their confidence. Parents should help their kids to join sports, music programs and other activities that can help your child feel confident, strong, alive and well.

There is much assistance for parents and families that are experiencing bullying. There are many resources that can turn your children around for the better instead of committing suicide. Parents need to support their kids and stand by them. Together they will put a stop to the bullying in school or everywhere that the bully is operating his or her activities of hatred towards other kids.

Parents are also advised to get involved with their kids at school. Bullying needs to be dealt with directly to stop hurtful behavior. All kids have the right to feel safe in their schools, homes and everywhere. Bullying is an

inappropriate behavior and is a behavior of hate, jealousy and wickedness. Bullying is an aggression and an exercise of control by the bully in order to maintain power over other innocent kids.

The innocent kids are abused every day in school. Bullying is a physically and psychologically harmful hurtful behavior. Parents should listen and respond as soon as possible to the complaint from their kids about the bullying. Bullying is a big problem that has injured many kids; bullying can make kids feels very bad. The stress of dealing with bullies could discourage kids from going to school.

A lot of bully kids are looking for attention. They might think it is the best way of being popular, or make believe that this is the way for them to be able to get what they want, or perhaps it makes them feel important. To them, this control also makes them feel important and powerful. Some bully kids come from families of domestic violence where shouting and screaming is going on from time to time, saying hurtful things to each other. Some bully kids copy what they see from their parents.

These kids who bully others don't care for other kid's feelings. They pick on some kids they are sure they can exercise their power over. They also pick on kids that they know are easily upset or depressed. They pick on kids that are more peaceful, and smarter in education than them. The worst thing about the bullying kids is that they pick on kids for practically no reason at all.

"Praise be to the God and Father of our Lord Jesus Christ, the Father of compassion and the God of all comfort, who comforts us in all our troubles, so that we can comfort those in any trouble with comfort we ourselves have received from God. For just as the sufferings of Christ flow over into our lives, so also through Christ our comfort overflows" (2nd Corinthians 1: 3-5). The word comfort means that God stands beside His children, encouraging and helping them in times of trouble. God supremely fulfills this role, for He sends to His children the Holy Spirit to comfort them. Apostle Paul learned during His service for the Lord how he had gone through many troubles that no suffering, however severe, can separate believers from the care and compassion of their heavenly Father.

In terms of raising kids, parents might experience or encounter circumstances that could weigh them down beyond human power of endurance, but they must not give up on their children. Parents must be very supportive of their children at all times; they must always see that raising kids is a full time job with so many complications and unforeseen circumstances. Prayer is a first hand tool that can help parents to achieve the goal of raising godly kids. Parents must ask God to help them in raising their kids in today's world of violence and all sorts of immoral behavior.

Lord Jesus Christ, we call unto You, we know that You call those who are burdened to come unto You. Bless the parents of the bully and the victim of the bully with Your healing power. Stretch out Your hand to heal them from all their emotional problems. Touch their spirit, soul and body with Your compassion. Touch them with your courage, mercy and love for themselves and for all other kids around them. With Your Holy hand, touch the bully's mind with Your great wisdom. Help them to grow up to live a godly life that will proclaim Your Holy name and praises. Teach the bully how to reach out and call unto You for everything they may need and help them to lead other children to know You our Lord. Turn the bully kids around to know Jesus' loving heart. Father, bless the children with good health in their inner most being. Bless them with strength, touch their life and create in them a new heart, a new spirit and a new name forever more. Amen.

Parents must pray for the youth suffering in the hands of the bullies, that are not only in school alone, but outside the school facilities. We must pray constantly that kids will be able to face the peer pressure and other forms of victimization from bullying. We must pray against suicide, and depression. Most importantly, we must pray against parents' denial and the denial of school teachers and other school officials. We must pray for the bully kids so that they know and realize what they are doing to other kids. May they may be made aware of the damage that they are doing in their own life and aware of the fact that they might end up in jail if they continue this violent behavior.

"Fear the Lord and the king, my son, and do not join with the rebellious, for those two will send sudden destruction upon them and who knows what calamities they can bring" (Proverbs 24:21-22).

BIBLICAL INDEX

Proverbs 10:1, 5-6, 11

Matthew 5:43-48

Proverbs 1: 8-9

Proverbs 2:1-5

Matthew 7:18

Proverbs 3:1-4

Psalm 25: 6-7

Proverbs 10:1, 6

Proverbs 22:1-2

Malachi 4:6

Exodus 10:2

Ephesians 6:1-3

Proverbs 4:1-7

Psalm 127: 3-5

Proverbs 24:1-4

2nd Corinthians 1:3-5

Proverbs 24: 21-22

BIBLIOGRAPHY

Believer's Bible Commentary, William MacDonald, Edited by Art Farstad, Thomas Nelson Publishers, Nashville, Atlanta, USA (1995 Edition)

The Interpretation of Scripture By James D. Smart, The Westminster Press, Philadelphia, USA October (2012)

The Student Bible, Philip Yancey and Tim Stafford, New Revised Standard Version, Published by Zondervan. Grand Rapids, Michigan USA (1994)

Books previously published by the author Grace Dola Balogun by Grace Religious Books Publishing & Distributors, Inc. New York:

PRAYER THE SOURCE OF STRENGTH FOR LIFE – English Edition

Prayer the Source of Strength for Life is a powerful book that will energize your spirit to pray more and more until the prayer is part of your life and until the gate of Heaven is opened and your prayer is answered. Your prayer life will change your life.

LA ORACION FUENTE DE FORTALEZA PARA LA VIDA – Spanish Edition.

Dios no's dio el poder de la oracion, quiere que lo usemos; debemos illamar, comunicarnos con el en todo lo que estemo spasando. El espera saber denosotros.

Spirit Power Volumes I and II

Spirit Power Volumes I and II both discuss the power of the Holy Spirit in the lives of Believers.

The Power of the Spirit of God begins from the creation of the world up until today. That power will also continue until Christ returns to reign. Hallelujah!

THE CROSS AND THE CRUCIFIXION

Our Lord Jesus Christ died on the Cross to bring forth love and compassion. Sin's impact on human life brings all other evil into our world, from one society to another society, from one culture to another.

But in Christ, we are clothed with His holiness. We have the gift of eternal life. The gate of Heaven is open and we are eligible for our inheritance in Heaven.

Hallelujah! Hosanna in the Highest. Jesus Christ paid it all, unto Him all we owe. The Cross of Christ is the Cross of joy, peace, and righteousness to all who believe in Him.

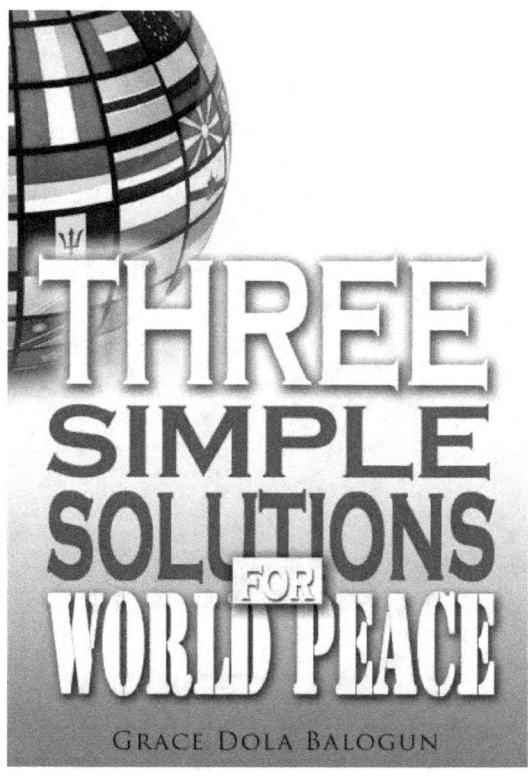

Three Simple Solutions for World Peace

Three Simple Solutions for World Peace is a book that clears all the confusion that many people of the world have been going through for many years. It is a book that gives light and advice to some of the problems that plague the world, and that offers solutions for these problems. It is a book that is full of knowledge, understanding and solutions that will bring some peace to the world.

JUSTIFICATION BY FAITH ALONE IN CHRIST ALONE

GRACE DOLA BALOGUN

Justification by Faith Alone in Christ Alone

Justification by Faith Alone in Christ Alone will clear all the confusion of believers' faith in Jesus Christ. Believers will also rejoice in the long-sufferings – they will rejoice in their sufferings, afflictions, persecutions, rejections and all various trials that may press in on them; because these long-sufferings will help all the believers to be redeemed in Christ.

CHRISTIAN CELL PHONE SERIES:

Christian Cell Phone Godly Wisdom helps readers understand the role of God's wisdom and the importance obtaining godly wisdom in one's life to produce prosperous results in all areas of life. These areas are critical and include family, relationships and finances. The acquiring of God's wisdom is to be sought after in life and will impact others as well.

Christian Cell Phone God's Favor is designed to give readers knowledge of God's favor from the Old Testament to the New Testament. With an analysis of the favor that was on Jesus the Son of God, the reader will find that God's favor can completely change one's life and lead others to Christ as well.

Christian Cell Phone God's Anointing takes a look at the anointing on the life of Jesus that includes present day believers in Christ Jesus. This anointing can be applied to all areas of life and can be seen in miraculous ways. The anointing is what makes our life incredible and supernatural, drawing all those who see, to Christ.

JESUS CHRIST THE JOY OF CHRISTMAS

Jesus Christ the Joy of Christmas gives praise and tribute to the child that was born in Bethlehem. Tracing the prophecies of Old about this King that was born, the author gives an account of the sinless lamb of God who came to take away the peoples' sin from a biblical perspective, who is the real Joy of Christmas.

About the Author

Grace Dola Balogun graduated from Fordham University Graduate School of Religion and Religious Education in the year 2010 with an M.A. in Religion and Religious Education. She has been a prayer mentor and advisor for many Christians of all denominations for many years.

Visit her online at:

www.Gracereligiousbookspublishers.com
Prayerstrengthforlife.com
Spiritpower.infosalvationcompleted.com Facebook
Twitter @prayersource

To order additional copies of this book, please E-mail: info@gracereligiousbookspublishers.com.

This book may also be ordered from 30,000 wholesalers, retailers, and booksellers in the U. S., and in Canada and over100 countries globally. To contact Grace Dola Balogun for an interview or a speaking engagement, please E-mail:

info@gracereligiousbookspublishers.com

The Spirit and the bride say,
"Come!" And let the one who hears say, "Come!" Let the
one who is thirsty come;
and let the one who wishes take the free
gift of the water of life (Revelation 22:17).

MARANATHA! COME, LORD JESUS!

www.ingramcontent.com/pod-product-compliance
Lightning Source LLC
Chambersburg PA
CBHW052057070526
44584CB00017B/2220